# THUNDERING STAMPEDE

## *The Chuckwagon Race*

Paul and Carol Easton

Johnson Gorman Publishers

*The Publishers*
Johnson Gorman Publishers
2003 – 35 Avenue SW
Calgary AB Canada T2T 2E2
info@jgbooks.com
www.jgbooks.com

*Credits*
Cover design by ArtPlus Limited.
Text design by Tannice Goddard, Soul Oasis Networking.
Special thanks to Jamie Heneghan for her work on the book.
Printed and bound in Canada by Friesens for Johnson Gorman Publishers.

*Acknowledgments*
Financial support provided by the Alberta Foundation for the Arts, a beneficiary of the Lottery Fund of the Government of Alberta.

COMMITTED TO THE DEVELOPMENT OF CULTURE AND THE ARTS

*National Library of Canada Cataloguing in Publication Data*
Easton, Paul A. (Paul Alexander), 1952–
Thundering stampede
ISBN 0-921835-61-2
1. Chuckwagon racing – Pictorial works. 1. Easton, Carol. 11. Title.
TS2025.E37 2002     791.8'4     C2002-910327-4

*Dedication*
For Emily and Nathan.

## Authors' Note

These pictures are a celebration of a wondrous cowboy sport, an extraordinary part of Western Canadian heritage. Even after many thousands of photographs, we remain inspired by the skill and dedication of the participants, both cowboys and horses. Chuckwagon racing is exhilarating.

Fortunately, you don't have to be a cowboy to appreciate this unique sport. The chuckwagon track is a long way from our day jobs in health care. But even as tenderfoot aficionados, we receive a warm welcome from the racers and their families.

It may seem odd that we didn't focus more on the cowboys that have won the most races or received the most accolades. In telling this story, we tried to include pictures of as many drivers and outriders as possible. For us, every driver and every outrider deserves star billing.

We also wanted to recognize another star group: the horses. Although we have not included the names of the horses in every racing photograph, each animal is named and cherished by its chuckwagon family. The cover photograph seems to show Mike Vigen with his red-shirted outriders in pursuit. Actually, the cover shows horses Sea, Grandpa, E.T., and Oak, plus a talented driver and his outriders, winning day money at the Calgary Stampede.

## Authors' Acknowledgments

We are indebted to some important folks who don't compete in the races. Our thanks to the officers and staff of the World Professional Chuckwagon Association, especially Arvilla Hess who helped us get started. And to Iris Glass for her promotion of our photographs. We are honored that author Glen Mikkelsen remembered our pictures and included them in his books. We are grateful for the assistance and encyclopedic knowledge of Billy Melville. We appreciate the business courage and editorial creativity of Dennis Johnson at Johnson Gorman publishing, who carried this project to its conclusion.

It may be of interest that all these photographs were taken with Nikon cameras and lenses.

# Contents

# Introduction

Horse racing. Steeplechase. Harness racing. Jumping. Bronc riding. Barrel racing. Sporting events involving horses are always impressive. But nothing can compare to the exhilaration of a chuckwagon race. Thundering wagons, fearless cowboys, and a stampede of horses from the foothills of the Rocky Mountains who continue racing right into old age. Horses with attitude, who are more likely to square dance than to jump over a faux brick wall.

Have you ever been to a chuckwagon race? Now's your chance to see one from an unparalleled perspective – through the lens of a camera. As you watch the race unfold through the photographs that follow, taste the danger, hear the thundering hooves, smell the mud in the air, and feel the drama and tension. Along the way, you'll meet the cowboys, their beloved thoroughbreds, and their families and fans, all of whom have dedicated their lives to this one-of-a-kind sport and to keeping the tradition and spirit of the Old West alive.

Enjoy the ride!

▲ Tyler Helmig wide open on the backstretch with horses Larr, Headache, Glo, and Jet. High River, June 22, 1997. (PAUL EASTON PHOTO)

◄ Duelling wagons. Reg Johnston (black jacket) and Kelly Sutherland (red jacket). Calgary Stampede, July 15, 2000. (CAROL EASTON PHOTO)

# Hotcakes to High Stakes

*In the foothills of the Rockies,*
*Four outfits make their way.*
*Wranglers, cows and wagons*
*Doing fifteen miles a day.*
*But the challenge stands before them*
*As the daytime turns to night:*
*Which outfit eats their supper first*
*And gets the best campsite.*

Chorus:
*From the days of the eighteen hundreds*
*All across the prairie lands*
*To the racetracks of the modern day*
*From Calgary to Cheyenne,*
*Well, the Old West has sure come alive*
*With the running of the wagon race:*
*Chuckwagon evolution from hotcakes to high stakes.*

Instrumental

*Cowboys still try to outdo each other*
*Like the way they've always done,*
*But instead of over fifteen miles*
*Today it's half of one.*
*Around an oval racetrack,*
*Where big dollars are their prize,*
*This modern sport is a race through hell,*
*Where the history still survives.*

Repeat chorus

**Not squeaky clean. Grant Profit and his team racing in the mud. High River, June 24, 2000.**
(PAUL EASTON PHOTO)

# CHAPTER ONE

# THE RACE
## Into the Barrel Turns

WELCOME TO THE CHUCKWAGON RACE: FOUR DRIVERS, FOUR WAGONS weighing a total of 5,300 pounds, 16 outriders, and 32 thoroughbreds squeezed onto a regular horse racetrack. In just over a minute of organized pandemonium, they'll start, turn a figure eight around their barrels in the infield, and gallop full-out around the five-eights of a mile track to the finish line. An enclosed stampede, this extreme sport is at once beautiful and dangerous.

Before the wagons can get onto the track, the cowboys and horses must contend with the infield – and especially the barrels. From a standing start, modern renditions of the historic cookstove and tent poles are tossed into the backs of the wagons by dismounted outriders as the wagons lurch forward. The wagons accelerate as they navigate the two barrels and shoot past the grandstand onto the racetrack, reaching full speed as they hit the backstretch. That's 45 miles per hour – and no seat belts or air bags. Meanwhile, in the midst of all the dust, the attending outriders for each wagon mount their galloping horses and follow the same figure-eight route onto the track.

It is in this confined infield space that the race is often won or lost. A movement before the horn sounds, a misdirected toss of a tent pole, a wrong turn, a misstep, an overturned barrel, a horse that departs without its outrider – any of these can incur penalties that can mean the race is lost even as it begins. But these riders and their thoroughbreds are seasoned professionals, the best in their sport, and truly costly mistakes are rare.

The infield is a scene of high-speed symmetry, simultaneous action, and four wagons cornering as if on rails. The scene is all fluid color and motion, choreographed so that the wagons finish their turns to run straight at the spectators in the packed grandstand – the perfect vantage point to watch a race.

Emotion at the start. Edgar Baptiste. Calgary Stampede, July 11, 1998. (CAROL EASTON PHOTO)

Starting positions. With the arena director mounted in the foreground, the wagons and outriders line up under the watchful eye of a cadre of judges. The red canvas turn-back barrier in the background will block the homestretch until the wagons have turned clockwise and left the infield. Calgary Stampede, July 9, 1995. (PAUL EASTON PHOTO)

The instant before the sound of the starter's klaxon is the calm before the storm. The rules require that the wagons be parked at the bottom barrel, facing the infield, with the horses held in place by the outriders. The apparent tranquillity before the start is deceiving. On a typical track, the race will unfold with frantic action lasting about 80 seconds. This is time zero. Thirty-two fidgeting thoroughbreds will explode in just a moment.

At the sound of the horn, the front outrider releases the bridle of the leaders and steps smartly back to steer them toward the top barrel.

**Outrider Quinn Dorchester holds the leaders for Ted Friesen with one hand while holding tight to the reins of his mount with the other to prevent it from galloping off at the sound of the horn. The wagon sits beside the bottom barrel. The team must charge forward and around the top barrel in the foreground. Tonight they are not lucky – they are starting in lane 2. That means it's farther to the inside rail, and they have farther to run than the wagon in lane 1. Strathmore, August 5, 2000. (CAROL EASTON PHOTO)**

*Paul & Carol Easton*

Then he runs with his outriding horse, which he must mount at a gallop – that is, if everything goes according to plan.

The strategy is to get all your team from standing start to full gallop before your competitors, all of whom have exactly the same intention. Of course, you can't use mental telepathy to tell your team of horses to run. Some drivers relay this urgency through the reins, some whistle, and others use descriptive terms that, thankfully, are lost in the commotion.

At once, each lead outrider needs to get clear of his wagon while remaining within his lane, mount his horse, and follow behind his wagon, all the while watching out for the other three wagons. The last task is especially important. The risk of being run over by a wagon is an occupational hazard.

Simultaneously, four outriders release the leaders, four drivers scream exhortations, and 16 wagon horses leap forward. To the uninitiated, the scene looks like bedlam. This is not a time for philosophic reflection.

**In the driver's seat, an excited cowboy communicates to his four adrenaline-pumped wagon horses that now is the time to take off. Simultaneously, outriders steadying the lead team jump out of the way. Drivers Jim Knight (in white), Ray Croteau (in red), Wayne Knight (in black), and outrider Roger Moore (in white). Calgary Stampede, July 7, 1996 (CAROL EASTON PHOTO)**

Troy Flad turns the top barrel. In theory, the other three horses in the team follow the path of the right front leader in an elegant figure eight around the barrels. That's in theory. As seen here, one rookie right-wheel horse is still unclear on the concept. Strathmore. August 5, 2000. (CAROL EASTON PHOTO)

Four leather reins from four thoroughbreds and only two strong, callused hands to guide them all. Harold Chapin, August 4, 2000. (PAUL EASTON PHOTO)

Within the confines of the infield, the wagon teams must execute a tight figure eight around two barrels, which are precisely located. To do that they shoot out from the bottom barrel, skim around the top barrel, and return on the opposite side of the bottom barrel, before hurtling out onto the oval track. The tighter a driver can "skin" the barrel without knocking it over, the quicker he can exit the infield and try to capture the coveted spot on the rail. Veterans who can carve around the barrels with lightning speed are called as master skinners.

Each great skinner has a signature hand position and rein technique to circumnavigate the barrels, and each horse knows its position in the team. Speedy skinning of the barrels is the product of countless hours of training and practice.

And by the way, how do drivers turn four horses either to the right or left with only four reins? They will tell you that each single rein turns the front (lead) and rear (wheel) horse on one side, either left or right.

Glen Ridsdale reins the leaders toward the top barrel. At first glance, the horses seem to be posing for the camera. Actually, their head positions are related entirely to the driver's efforts on the reins to prevent them from running over the next barrel. If they hit the barrel, the race is lost as it begins. Strathmore, August 4, 1997. (PAUL EASTON PHOTO)

Neal Walgenbach's horses may look like they're about to fall, but these acrobatics will result in a perfect, quick figure eight around the barrels. These are four of the best-trained, most pampered horses on earth. Calgary. Stampede, July 9, 2000. (CAROL EASTON PHOTO)

From the stands, only the most knowledgeable chuckwagon fan can discern the techniques each driver uses to navigate around the barrels. In a matter of seconds, the teams are storming out of the infield and onto the track.

Floyd Bradshaw rounds the 2 barrel. To most of the participants and spectators, the frenetic activity at the barrel is a blur. Strathmore, August 5, 2000. (PAUL EASTON PHOTO)

*Paul & Carol Easton*

If the barrel is skinned too tightly, a horse or wagon may clip it, so as a safety measure, the barrels are constructed of light, flexible plastic. The only damage done is to the cowboy's ego as he incurs a time penalty that most times ensures that his team will lose the race.

**Honest, there *is* a plan. John Lumsden has completed half of the figure eight. The team is heading back to the bottom (starting) barrel in the foreground, although that's not obvious from this perspective. Trout Springs, June 17, 1995. (CAROL EASTON PHOTO)**

Sorting out the infield activity is easier if you know the dress code. Each team including driver and outriders wears the same color jacket. And each color corresponds to a barrel and lane number, which is determined before the race by lottery. The team racing around the number 1 barrels is always attired in white while those racing around barrels 2, 3, and 4 wear red, black, and yellow.

This seeming chaos can be explained. The speediest wagon (with the green tarp) has completed the turn around the top barrel and is flying back toward the starting barrel to complete its figure eight in the infield. Two other wagons are still negotiating their top barrels, while all of the outriders are trying to mount their enthusiastic thoroughbreds that intend to gallop around the barrels themselves. Buddy Bensmiller (in the wagon with the green tarp), Jason Glass (in the checkerboard wagon), and Mike Vigen (in the black wagon). Calgary Stampede, July 7, 1996. (PAUL EASTON PHOTO)

A perfect turn around the barrels has symmetry. The team is in line, the reins are firm, and the outriders are getting mounted quickly behind the wagon so they can stay close to it throughout the race.

A lovely day, perfect form, a glorious vista. But Jerry Bremner and his team aren't admiring the scenery as they accelerate back to the bottom starting barrel. Ponoka Stampede, July 1993. (PAUL EASTON PHOTO)

In about 15 seconds from the sound of the horn, all the wagons will have circled the barrels and exited the infield. If the wagon has been loaded properly, if the barrels are still standing, and if no other time infraction has occurred, a team has a hope of winning the race.

Oops. These wagons have completed their figure–eight barrel turns and are galloping out of the infield onto the racetrack. Alas, Floyd Bradshaw's 1 barrel is headed over, resulting in a five–second penalty that virtually guarantees that his team will lose the race today. Drivers Floyd Bradshaw (in white), Jason Johnstone (in red), and Todd Baptiste (in black) getting out of the infield. Strathmore, August 1, 1999. (PAUL EASTON PHOTO)

Cam Shaurette's team splashes through ankle–deep mud. His wagon leaves a lovely rooster tail of mud as it slaloms out of the infield. So far, the driver's shirt is still white, and the horses are still brown. But not for long! Just wait. In about 30 seconds, there won't be a clean shirt, face, or horse anywhere in sight. Ponoka Stampede, June 28, 1998. (CAROL EASTON PHOTO)

By the end of the race, Norm Cuthbertson will be covered in mud, except for his hat, which is covered by a plastic protector. Norm is accompanied by outrider Brian Mayan. High River, June 24, 2000. (CAROL EASTON PHOTO)

Conditions, however, are sometimes far from perfect. If rain falls on wagon race day, the race will go on, but infield times will be longer in the mud. If the track is really muddy, the rules change. For the safety of horses and outriders the outriders are excused except for a single cowboy on foot to steady the lead team until the horn.

Nobody likes to race in the mud, but once the drivers have checked the track and confirmed that beneath the sloppy mud the track base is firm and safe for the horses, the show goes on. Cowboys may not like the mud, but it doesn't stop them. After the race, the drivers and horses get cleaned up.

# CHAPTER TWO

# THE DRIVERS
## Celebrity Skinners & Racers

**W**HAT DO YOU NEED TO BE A WAGON RACER? FOR A START, A TEAM OF thoroughbreds, portable canvas barns, a wagon, and axle grease. And a sponsor willing to foot the bill. Then training, training, and more training.

You need to convince your four racehorses to sprint in a tight figure eight around two barrels and gallop five-eights of a mile while pulling a 1,325 pound wagon. Then you must be ready to load horses and equipment onto a transport, drive overnight, and practice at 5:00 A.M. the next morning, traveling for the entire summer across the West.

When you gather two or three dozen teams, including the barn crews, families and outriders in their trucks and motorhomes, it's a caravan. For a few days each year, each racetrack sprouts a tent city. And then they're gone until next season.

Who are the people who actually live like this? Why do they risk life and limb for what is peanuts in the world of professional sport? These few cowboys and their close-knit families are on the road for four months every year because they are passionate about this extreme sport and dedicated to the western heritage it represents. Many of them have been raised with wagon racing in their blood – "born to eat wagon dust," as they say. They are extraordinary characters – you've gotta love 'em!

The caravan has arrived, the barns are set up, and the race preparations are complete. It's just before dusk, and the grandstand has filled with race fans. All that remains is for one of the local girls to sing the national anthem (country and western style) and for the drivers to be introduced to the crowd. This is about the only time you'll ever catch all these cowboys with their hats off.

Out of the dust. . . . In a previous vocation, Mark Sutherland was responsible for a classroom of students. Medicine Hat, June 10, 2001. (CAROL EASTON PHOTO)

The color of their jacket identifies the barrel number that drivers have drawn for the race. Facing the grandstand, (from right to left) Bob Van Eaton, Don Chapin, Phil Pollack, Colt Cosgrave, Kevin Baird, Leonard DeLaronde, Troy Flad, Dave Shingoose, Jess Willard, and John Lumsden remove their hats for the national anthem. Strathmore, August 2, 1997. (CAROL EASTON PHOTO)

In Ian Tyson's "Half a Mile of Hell," a chuckwagon racing anthem, he sings:

> *Ron Glass and Hally Walgenbach,*
> *They were skinners to the man,*
> *On up to Kelly Sutherland,*
> *And the Dorchesters as well . . .*
>
> *Hear the thunder of the hoof beats,*
> *It's a sound they know so well . . .*

(Music & Lyrics copyright © 1978 Ian Tyson, from *One Jump Ahead of the Devil*, Stony Plain Records. Used with permission.)

Wagon racing is a family tradition. The son of legendary Ron Glass, Tom Glass, (in black) duels driver Buddy Bensmiller (in red) and out-riders Jim Shield (red helmet) and Wayne Wright (pink helmet) on the backstretch at High River, the home track of the Glass clan. High River, June 15, 1996. (PAUL EASTON PHOTO)

The heroes in the song are not fictional characters. Ron Glass passed the chuckwagon racing tradition to son Tom, who accumulated more than 25 victories and championships in a career spanning over 37 years. Until Tom Glass's retirement, it was common to see his son Jason racing against his dad in the same heat. Chuckwagon racing sinks its roots deep.

Kelly Sutherland also travels and races alongside his son Mark. The Dorchesters are another family that has been chuckwagon racing for generations. Although Dallas Dorchester has retired from competition, he can still be seen driving a demonstration heat at the Calgary Stampede before the competitors take to the track. Dallas Dorchester inherited his father's lucky cowboy hat, and the hat is still racing, today, worn by Dallas's nephew, driver Troy Dorchester.

**Kelly Sutherland (in black) and Dallas Dorchester (in white) on the back-stretch. The hat Dallas is wearing in this picture is not the family-heirloom lucky hat. Bad luck for this race. High River, June 1992. (CAROL EASTON PHOTO)**

Chuckwagon drivers may spend their summers on the road following the circuit, but in the off-season they don't hit the golf links like so many other professional sport stars. Many turn to more mundane pursuits to earn a living on Hollywood movie sets and cattle ranches, and in school classrooms, the oil patch, executive suites and veterinarians' offices.

The veterinarian, Dr. Doyle Mullaney, is in — the wagon box, not the office. Doyle is often introduced as the "Official Irishman of Chuckwagon racing," and his wagon box features a lucky leprechaun. Although a little luck is welcome, after 34 years of racing, this wily professional doesn't leave much to chance. Ponoka Stampede, June 29, 1996. (**PAUL EASTON PHOTO**)

*Paul & Carol Easton*

The dedication of wagon racing families to their sport is not deterred by danger or tragedy. Fortunately, serious accidents are rare. But even the tragic loss of a chuckwagon racer is usually followed by a son or nephew stepping into the wagon to carry on the tradition. These are matters of fate and honor. These cowboys are real.

You turn a lot of barrels in 25 years of wagon racing. Veteran professional driver Don Chapin and his team demonstrate just how to do it. Don Chapin once ran an entire season of racing without a single miscalculation – without even one second in penalties – a feat not likely to be repeated. Edmonton Northlands Park, July 26, 1999. (PAUL EASTON PHOTO)

Kevin Baird is the picture of concentration. Ponoka Stampede, June 3, 1993. (PAUL EASTON PHOTO)

Rick Fraser (in red), Glen Ridsdale (in white), and Wayne Knight (in yellow). Calgary Stampede, July 12, 2000. (CAROL EASTON PHOTO)

When the race heats up on the oval, each driver has a unique style. Some drivers never flinch or betray the slightest emotion. They could be out for a peaceful drive in the park, except for great clods of mud flying the air around them as they gallop out of the infield.

Other competitors are exuberant, throwing the reins, screaming exhortations to their horses, assuming they will actually be heard over the roar of the crowd. By the time the wagons round the last corner and turn back toward the grandstand, emotion is at a peak. For every driver, this is the most fun he can have with his boots on!

This skinner looks like nothing so much as a mud statue. Calgary Stampede, July 1993.
(PAUL EASTON PHOTO)

The racing season starts next week, so Grant and Shelley Profit and outrider Jason Lemieux get in some practice. Here, the co-pilot/starter is the driver's spouse. Hayworth Stables track, May 20, 2000.
(PAUL EASTON PHOTO)

By the time the race is finally over, everything may look a little hazy through the driver's racing goggles. But no driver will miss a wagon race just because he might get a little dirty.

The controlled high-speed action of race day does not happen automatically. Even a clever thoroughbred has to learn the complexities of a figure eight. So, before you can win, it's practice, practice. Successful chuckwagon outfits are often composed of dedicated racing families whose members all contribute.

Despite caution, training, and professionalism, wagon racing is hard-edged competition. And just like auto racing, *stuff* happens. If something goes very wrong, the pain can be very real.

Like any racing sport, chuckwagon racing can be dangerous. The drivers are in danger of being thrown from the wagon and crushed beneath wagon wheels and horses' hooves. The outriders are in danger of head injuries if they're thrown from their horses, and the horses are at risk of bone fractures and heart attacks. But this is a modern professional sport, and the participants know that their lives and the safety of their beloved horses depend upon avoiding accidents.

**Look closely – Harold McCarthy's wagon has only three wheels! Now you've seen everything. Wagon wheels are not supposed to fall off, and, in theory, a wagon with only three wheels should tip over. If only this had happened during practice, this driver could have had a private laugh. But now he's in front of 25,000 fans, and there's a television camera. . . . Calgary Stampede, July 8, 1997. (PAUL EASTON PHOTO)**

Much has changed throughout the years to improve safety in wagon racing. The infield is spacious, and the new tracks are banked, multi-layered feats of engineering that provide perfect horse footing. And if track conditions are too sloppy for sure footing, these cowboys won't even let their horses race. Strict rules now govern the weight of the wagon and the stove, barrels have given way to collapsible rubber and plastic imitations, aspiring drivers must be formally accredited, and the time penalties for minor wagon interference are so costly that any infraction guarantees the loss of the race. These cowboys are serious about safety.

Nevertheless, accidents do happen. Chuckwagon racing is a genuine extreme sport that involves real danger. Not everyone gets a chance to retire.

**Larry McEwen rounds the third corner as his father's wagon, driverless, follows in the background. The wagon without a driver had been driven by Bill McEwen. A veteran racer and a loving father and grandfather, he died of injuries sustained in this race. Calgary Stampede, July 9, 1999.**
(CAROL EASTON PHOTO)

# The Chuckwagon Prayer

Richard Cosgrave, two-time Calgary Stampede aggregate winner and recipient of the Calgary Stampede's prestigious Guy Weadick Award. A passionate racer and devoted father, he died of racing injuries on August 13, 1993. High River, June 1992. **(PAUL EASTON PHOTO)**

*Here we are again today*
*Risking our lives for very little pay*
*But it's the life we choose*
*And the life we shall live,*
*And Lord we don't ask anyone to give.*

*But we just want to thank You*
*For the many trouble free miles we travel each year;*
*Up and down the highways and dusty old roads*
*Knowing that you're near.*

*Now, we ain't always been straight,*
*Or taken a religious stand,*
*But when we crawl upon the seat of that wagon*
*And look back at the family,*
*There's someone we truly believe in*
*And you're the Man.*

*And when we turn them barrels*
*And she lifts up on two,*
*I sometimes hear a little voice saying,*
*"Don't worry son, 'cause I'm in here too."*

*In the past you have taken a few drivers*
*And a few outriders, even the odd child or two;*
*But really, Lord, no one has really ever blamed you.*

*So we don't ask that you take us to Heaven*
*Or never run in stormy weather,*
*But when it's all over*
*And you gather us into your mighty Kingdom Come*
*Would you please keep us*
*All together.*

*Amen.*

Wrecks. Obituaries. The risks should be terrifying. But the cowboys' love of the sport transcends the risk. At the end of the day, when the racing is done, they have no regrets. And, oh, those how aches and pains melt away when a team crosses the finish line first. Those hard-earned victories feel so good!

George Normand, a six-time world champion, a classy cowboy and gentleman racer, died of racing injuries on July 2, 1994. The trademark racing symbol from his wagon remains on the track to this day, carried on in his memory by a friend. Ponoka Stampede, June 1993. (CAROL EASTON PHOTO)

Breaking into the sport can be tough if a driver doesn't come from a chuckwagon racing family. These drivers often start as outriders and then face the daunting task of buying a wagon and equipment and piecing together a team of wagon racing horses. To get started, they need to "bet the farm." But they do it. Then they have to earn their accreditation to join the racing circuit.

Roger Moore receives the Orville Strandquist Best Rookie Driver Award from Hall of Fame cowboy Orville himself (in the red jacket). After years of tough races as an outrider, Roger Moore scratched together enough money to buy his own team of horses and get a wagon. Then came his first coveted invitation to race at the granddaddy of all wagon races, the Calgary Stampede. Now, wearing his signature coonskin cap, he accepts the trophy in front of thousands of race fans. How sweet it is. Calgary Stampede, July 12, 1997. (CAROL EASTON PHOTO)

As rookies struggle to get established in the sport, they look for inspiration and advice from the champions. Kelly Sutherland is one of the greatest. Nine-time World and nine-time Calgary Stampede champion, he has driven to victory on virtually every track in 35 years of wagon racing. He's mentioned in Ian Tyson's wagon tribute. As track announcers say, "They call him the King when he's doing his thing." In the sport of chuckwagon racing, he's Wayne Gretzky on wheels.

**Champion chuckwagon driver Kelly Sutherland (with his trademark eagle feather pointing down from his cowboy hat) with outriders Rick Fraser (white hat) and Lyle Panbrum (black hat), is congratulated by Bruce Watson, president of the World Professional Chuckwagon Association on winning his seventh World Chuckwagon Championship. Strathmore, August 3, 1998. (CAROL EASTON PHOTO)**

CHAPTER THREE

# THE OUTRIDERS
## Essential Supporting Cast

Because outriders perform in the shadow of the wagons, few photographs of them have been published. But they are real showmen, revered even by other cowboys as brilliant riders, wily horsemen, and top-notch athletes. They don't just ride along with the wagons. Wagon racing is a team sport, and the brilliance or blunders of outriders often determine the outcome of the race.

The dangers facing an outrider are legion. Throughout each race there is always the risk of being thrown from an unfamiliar mount at full gallop and being run over by the chuckwagons or or crushed between them. In addition, outriders assist the driver with the wagon horses, which means helping muddy horses to their feet, reining in runaways, and diving into tangles of reins to prevent injury to the horses. For the outriders, all this is a risky business.

Like the drivers, the outriders are an eclectic group. They come from a diverse range of occupations including accountants, paramedics, salesmen, university students, flight attendants, models, equine therapists, movie stuntmen, and retired bull riders. But when chuckwagon season rolls around, they're all just cowboys doing what they love best. Before a race they'll often be seen clowning around to calm those pre-race jitters.

They bring strong rivalry to the track, since they are members of opposing chuckwagon teams, and they also compete directly with one another for the coveted Outrider Championship awarded at the end of the season. But after the races, this is a tight-knit group. They share the admiration of the fans as well as the dangers on the track. Friendship and cooperation among competitors are crucial in a sport this dangerous.

Reflecting with rein in mouth. . . . **Eddie Melville, Calgary Stampede, June 13, 1998. (CAROL EASTON PHOTO)**

(From left to right) Eddie Melville, Quinn Dorchester, Eugene Jackson, Gary Mayan, Dallas Mullaney, Jim Shield, Brian Mayan, Ernie Jimmy, Trevor Parenteau, Gary Lauder, and Lyle Panbrum (lying under the black hat) show their camaraderie before a race. Ponoka Stampede, June 29, 1995. (CAROL EASTON PHOTO)

Two-time Calgary Stampede champion outrider Eugene Jackson, affectionately known as "Action Jackson." June 1994. A great outrider, fine friend, and Alberta First Nations' member, he died of racing injuries sustained July 11, 1996. (PAUL EASTON PHOTO)

Many outriders now wear flak jackets and helmets, but the danger is still very real.

A cigarette and a little limbering up help calm pre-race nerves. Butch Stewart. Ponoka Stampede, June 29, 1995. (PAUL EASTON PHOTO)

Before the race begins, the front outrider holds the leaders (the front pair of wagon horses) and his own thoroughbred until the horn sounds. Then he steps back to get out of the way before the wagon horses charge. The next challenge is to get onto his own horse and stay close to the wagon.

At the sound of the horn, at the back of the wagon, two more outriders load the tent pegs and fly while a fourth outrider loads the 10-pound "cookstove." (As a safety feature, the "stove" is now lightweight plastic.) Throughout this process, it's crucial that the outriders keep a firm grip on the reins of their own mounts because they will need to gallop after the wagon once it's loaded.

**Doug Irvine, Dave Biever, and Gary Lauder load the tent pegs and stove into the back of Brian Laboucane's wagon. Calgary Stampede, July 9, 1995. (CAROL EASTON PHOTO)**

Here, both horse and outrider are off the ground. He did not learn this in riding school. Despite a great mount, this cowboy will probably incur a late-outrider penalty, since he's still attempting to mount his galloping horse even after it has passed the barrels onto the track. Calgary Stampede, July 11, 2000. (CAROL EASTON PHOTO)

Shawn Calf Robe mounts his horse. Note that he doesn't use the stirrups at all, but leaps straight into the saddle. Strathmore, August 2, 1999. (PAUL EASTON PHOTO)

After the outriders have done their duty holding and loading the wagon, they too must run the race, beginning with the figure eight in the infield. However, there is a small problem to resolve before they can gallop away. They are still on foot! Their race begins by mounting a horse that is already charging after the wagon. There are several variations of the amazing flying-mount-onto-a-galloping-horse manoeuvre. Please do not attempt any of these at home.

And don't think that these horses and outriders have practiced together. The outriders' horses are provided by the chuckwagon teams, and the outriders may never have ridden their horses before this race. A good outrider must be able to size up his mount at a glance.

Brian Mayan at full gallop approaching the fourth corner. Lethbridge, June 18, 1998.
(CAROL EASTON PHOTO)

Okay, almost onto those galloping horses. Now to catch up to the wagons. . . . And yes, he is wearing running shoes. In a matter of safety and agility taking priority over tradition and style, many outriders are not fashionably attired in lizard skin cowboy boots. Similarly, many of the cowboy hats have been replaced with helmets. Wayne Wright (in black) and Lyle Panbrum (in white) leave the infield. Ponoka Stampede, June 29, 1996.
(PAUL EASTON PHOTO)

Through the camera lens, a single outrider at the fleeting moment when all four of his horse's hooves are tucked in gallop is a thing of beauty. But to an outrider, a solitary ride is not a pretty picture because that usually means his horse is running far behind the wagons. Unless the rider can catch up before the finish line, he will incur a one-second penalty for the team, and in chuckwagon racing one second is a long, long time. With a late outrider it won't matter that the chuckwagon had a great running time. Chuckwagon racing is, above all, a team sport.

An experienced outrider is always in demand. Since there can be as many as a dozen heats in a night of wagon racing, in theory an outrider can race for a dozen teams per night. That's a bunch of unfamiliar horses to ride competitively in an evening. Typically, an accomplished outrider will be invited to ride for most races. Rookie riders will have more spare time on their hands.

A typical day at work for a wagon outrider. Here, two red-shirted outriders from one team and two black-shirted riders from an opposing team follow the wagons. Sure, there may be a tiny amount of dust. (From left to right) two-time World Champion outrider Dale Gray, Gary Mayan, and Lyle Panbrum ride through the dust. High River, June 15, 1997. (CAROL EASTON PHOTO)

The ideal position for the outriders on the oval is wide and outside, as far away from the wagons as they can get while still remaining within a few lengths of the wagons. The most dangerous route around the track for an outrider is in the midst of the wagons and close to the inside rail.

Here riders from three teams (identified by their black, yellow, and red shirts) travel in relative safety between the last wagon and the outside rail. (From left to right) Gary Mayan, Trevor Parenteau, Ernie Jimmy, Jim Shield, and Cam Shaurette. High River, June 16, 1996. (CAROL EASTON PHOTO)

Even on the largest tracks with more wagons and outriders, the same principle applies: try to travel safely behind and outside the last wagon. With outriders in a large pack, the drivers may not be sure how close their outriders are to the wagon.

The four white shirted outriders closest to this wagon actually belong to a wagon that is well ahead of the photo. (From left to right) Quinn Dorchester, Reo King, Wayne Wright, Brian Mayan, Shawn Calf Robe, Ross Knight, Sandy MacKenzie, Darren Mitsuing, Clen Weeseekase, and Doug Irvine race in a tight pack behind Stu Napper's wagon. Calgary Stampede, July 1999. (CAROL EASTON PHOTO)

*Paul & Carol Easton*

An outrider must not get too far behind. Each rider must be within 150 feet of his wagon when it crosses the finish line to avoid a costly time penalty. Since many races are won or lost on a fraction of a second, tardy outriders are unpopular. And with infield penalties as severe as four seconds for failure to load a stove or two seconds for an outrider knocking over a barrel, clumsy outriders have a short career.

The view an outrider never wants to see. Dale Gray (blue and red helmet), Wayne Wright (pink and white helmet), and Shawn Calf Robe (red and white helmet) set up for the stretch drive. Calgary Stampede, July 12, 2000. (CAROL EASTON PHOTO)

The outriders receive the same pay per race – $75 – rain or shine. The good news is they don't have to wash the horses.

Despite the high risk and low pay, the life of an outrider has appeal. After the race, these athletes are done for the day. Since they are independent of the wagon racing teams, they are usually spared the hours of post-race work caring for the horses and maintaining the wagons and equipment.

At the end of the last race of the day, the outriders parade in front of the grandstand and tip their hats or helmets to the crowd before riding the horses to the barns. Meanwhile, the announcer intones some corny warning to the crowd about safeguarding their daughters. After the race, outriders become the infamous cowboys of the wagon circuit. Itinerant and a little on the wild side, their jeans fit tight.

**Choices. If you don't wear your goggles, you can't see. If you wear your goggles, you still can't see. (From left to right) Troy Bell, Quinn Dorchester, Wayne Wright, and Dale Gray in a mud shower. High River, June 26, 2000. (PAUL EASTON PHOTO)**

*Paul & Carol Easton*

The traditional outrider salute – though it doesn't often include a pink haired cowboy! (From left to right) Quinn Dorchester, Sandy MacKenzie, Wayne Wright, Brian Mayan, and Roger Moore salute the crowd. Calgary Stampede, July 11, 2000. (PAUL EASTON PHOTO)

If it gets really muddy, the outriders are excused, except to hold the leaders at the start of the race. Guess this isn't quite bad enough. Cam Shaurette. Calgary Stampede, July 7, 1995. (CAROL EASTON PHOTO)

# CHAPTER FOUR

# THE RACE
## Around the Track

▲ Reg Johnstone and team coming straight at you. Calgary Stampede, July 11, 1999. (PAUL EASTON PHOTO)

**N**OW THAT THE WAGONS AND OUTRIDERS HAVE CLEARED THE INFIELD, they're free of their lanes and can grab the best available position on the track. No more fancy turns. Now it's a horserace. Since all the horses are fast, tactics are important.

The lucky driver who drew barrel and lane number 1 should get the rail, for a shortest, quickest sprint around the track. His strategy also is the simplest. Just run hard and "clean," avoiding all penalties. Unless, of course, another wagon turns the barrels like a rocket sled and grabs the rail away from the driver on barrel 1. Coming out of the infield, stealing the rail position is on everyone's mind.

If your competitor is ahead on the rail, then it's decision time: either tuck in on the rail behind the lead wagon and hope for an opening later, or move to the center of the track and try to stay with 'em. It's a brave driver who decides to stay on the outside and trust his horses to run a longer race and still win. Sometimes, of course, the outside may be the only position left so the only strategy is to take the long way home.

The first turn holds a special excitement as high-speed congestion occurs. With four wagon teams vying aggressively for the coveted rail, things can get very crowed very quickly. Drivers won't put their teams at serious risk, but that doesn't prevent them from a certain amount of jostling and brinkmanship. The first corner is not for the fainthearted and often can be a scene as chaotic as the infield run around the barrels.

◀ Doug Green hollers as his team careens into the first corner. This is a prairie dog's perspective of an approaching chuckwagon that has just left the infield and is entering the first corner at full throttle. An actual prairie dog would be in very serious trouble about now. Ponoka Stampede, June 30, 1998. (PAUL EASTON PHOTO)

By the time the wagons round the first corner, only about 20 seconds of the race have elapsed. Depending on the rail position and the number of upset barrels lying back in the infield, one wagon may already be at a huge disadvantage.

**The driver in the foreground looks like he's winning. He's not. He's ahead for the moment but not nearly far enough in the lead to swing in and steal the rail. The driver on the rail is behind but holds a tactical advantage. Drivers Don Chapin (in black) and Troy Dorchester (in white) negotiate the first corner. Medicine Hat, June 13, 1999. (CAROL EASTON PHOTO)**

After evenly matched infield figure eights, drivers Kelly Sutherland (in black), Hugh Sinclair (in red), and Neil Walgenbach (in white) run three-wide into the first corner during the final heat. The inside wagon isn't about to cede the rail position. For the hapless wagon on the outside, this will be a long five-eights of a mile run unless he chooses to drop back and follow on the rail. Neil Walgenbach, who snagged the rail, won the race and the show. Medicine Hat Exhibition and Stampede, June 1999. (PAUL EASTON PHOTO)

When the wagons reach the second corner, they are usually separated with one or two wagons leading and the other wagons tucked in behind on the rail, waiting for an opening to take the lead.

Already on the second corner, this driver looks like he still has the rail all to himself. But if you look more closely, you'll notice the cloud of dust ahead of his lead horse. Art Nabe is not lucky this time; another wagon is ahead of him on the rail. High River, June 1993. (PAUL EASTON PHOTO)

The second turn is followed by the backstretch – the equine drag strip. It's a place where a driver may decide to go for it and "just smoke 'em." Well, maybe – that's the plan anyway. Whatever the drivers' tactics, the backstretch is often a place of intense wheel-to-wheel action.

**Don Chapin takes command of the backstretch with outrider Eugene Jackson in hot pursuit. High River, June 15, 1996. (PAUL EASTON PHOTO)**

Most spectators see the race from the grandstand on the infield, so the drag race down the backstretch is only distant motion. But let the camera take you closer. Let the wagons run directly at you. For some chuckwagon aficionados, this is the most exhilarating perspective. For an instant, all the horses seem suspended in air, then they loom larger and roar on by.

Roy David about halfway through the Half Mile of Hell. High River, June 1995. (CAROL EASTON PHOTO)

*Paul & Carol Easton*

As the wagons careen down the backstretch, they really do rumble like thunder. Sixteen wagon horses pounding the ground, 16 wheels churning up dust, four drivers yelling – usually at the horses, but occasionally at one another. And up to 16 outriders following in the dust.

By the time the wagons near the end of the backstretch, one team has usually slipped into the lead. It's a lucky day when, after all this galloping, two or more wagons are still running neck and neck. The perfect vision of a "four-wide" is as rare as a hen's tooth.

**Dave Shingoose (in black), Cam Shaurette (in yellow), Glen Boychuk (in red), and Phil Pollack (in white) run nearly four wide. In wagon–speak a four–wide is that very rare moment when 16 horses run shoulder to shoulder. High River, June 25, 1995. (PAUL EASTON PHOTO)**

By the time the wagons reach the end of the backstretch, the race has been on for about 50 seconds. If no wagon has pulled into the lead, things can get very interesting on the third corner. . . .

This driver is exactly where he wants to be. Doug Irvine leads at the end of the backstretch and holds the rail. He ought to win this race, provided that all the barrels are still standing in the infield. Calgary Stampede, July 18, 1999. (PAUL EASTON PHOTO)

*Paul & Carol Easton*

A pack of wagons and outriders heading into the third turn. One wagon has a slight lead, but there's a long way to go. Dr. Doyle Mullaney (in black), Kevin Baird (in red), Grant Profit (in yellow), and Hugh Sinclair (in white) approach the third turn. Strathmore, August 3, 1998. (CAROL EASTON PHOTO)

Although two-thirds of the race has elapsed, nobody has won it yet. Perhaps one driver has been holding his team back for a dash to the finish. Maybe some of these horses are wily old racers who won't light the afterburners until the screaming fans in the grandstand get closer.

Still too close to call. Two veteran drivers. Great horses. One team is ahead, but the other is still on the rail. Don't bet on the outcome. Ward Willard (in red) and Dr. Doyle Mullaney (in white) battle on the third corner. High River, June 26, 1993. (PAUL EASTON PHOTO)

The lead can still change. Anything can still happen. The fans are cheering wildly for their favorites, and the horses are running flat out. After corner three comes the final dash to the finish line.

Ron David (in white) and Troy Dorchester (in red) coming out of the third corner. Lethbridge, June 18, 1999. (PAUL EASTON PHOTO)

CHAPTER FIVE

# THE HORSES
## *Equine Athletes & Wagons*

*T*HE EQUINE ATHLETES OF THE WAGON RACING WORLD LIVE THE DREAM OF a thoroughbred: they're pampered like family pets, housed in portable barns, cared for with loving attention, and get to run to their heart's desire until they're geriatric. Speedy youngsters carry outriders, brawny adults pull right in front of the wagon, and wizened veterans set the course around the barrels. When the racing is finally over, these retired champions go to pasture in the majestic foothills of the Rockies. For a thoroughbred, chuckwagon racing is horsy heaven.

In the 250-years history of the breed, the thoroughbred has flaunted its power and grace in many different types of racing, but chuckwagon racing must surely rank as one of the most extraordinary of thoroughbred races. Horses running not just singly but in teams. Not just carrying riders on their backs but pulling wagons. The characteristics of a great wagon thoroughbred are more complex than in other forms of thoroughbred racing.

After camp is set up, the endless task of caring for a whole stable of horses begins. Feed 'em, brush 'em, wash 'em, tend to the hooves, and shovel up the potpourri. And these horses have other equipment, beginning with their racing wheels, the chuckwagons. The wagons need unloading, washing, and axle grease. At least you don't have to shovel up after a wagon.

▲ **The chuckwagon equivalent of a carwash. Ponoka, June 13, 1993.** (CAROL EASTON PHOTO)

◄ **A kitchen for the horses. Blue barrels for water, red buckets for oats, and a wheelbarrow and pitchfork to clean up after the meal. Horses are really messy eaters. Ponoka Stampede, July 2, 2000.** (CAROL EASTON PHOTO)

Local veterinarians and animal care specialists are needed for a few days to support the city of pampered horses that has sprung up overnight.

Someone came up with the great idea of posting the wagon camp directory on the corral fence. Royal and Regal discover that the backing is tasty and decide to make lunch out of it. Ponoka, July 2, 2000. (CAROL EASTON PHOTO)

A competitor gets a new set of shoes. The artisan swinging the hammer is a farrier. In just one season, a great racing horse goes through more pairs of shoes than Imelda Marcos. Ponoka Stampede, June 29, 1996. (PAUL EASTON PHOTO)

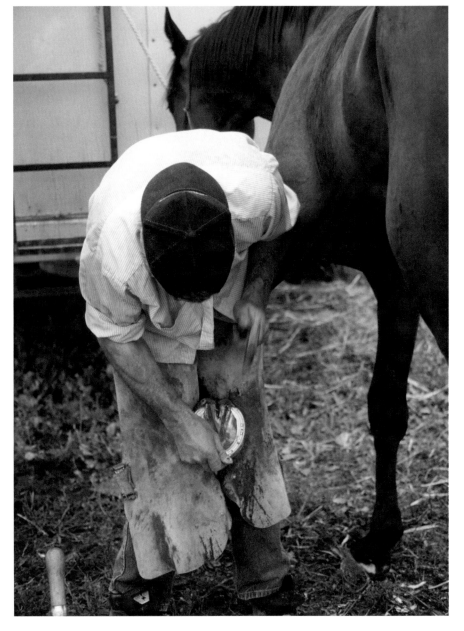

*Paul & Carol Easton*

Iris Glass gives Nova a reward for a hard day's work while Cole Bain and Roll Tide look on. They are unconcerned that the lady with the bucket is the reigning grand dame of chuckwagon racing and the matriarch of a clan of wagon racing champions. From the equine point of view, she's a familiar source of tasty treats. High River, June 1992. (CAROL EASTON PHOTO)

Nordic, an outriding horse from the Hugh Sinclair stable, gets cooled off. This impromptu barefoot horse shower is typical pampering on a hot summer day. He's a star wagon horse, but he's also a family pet. Ponoka Stampede, July 2, 2000. (PAUL EASTON PHOTO)

Anticipation . . . it's almost race time. Bring on the saddles. A horse groomer gets his team of outrider horses ready for the big race. Ponoka Stampede, July 1, 1993. (PAUL EASTON PHOTO)

Okay, brush 'em before and after practice and the race. Give them a shower after the race and again if they roll in the dust. Repeat with each of 16 horses. Then start over the next day. After the race, the horses need to be walked and cooled and shooed away from the water bucket. Then there's ointment and cover and tender loving care for any little scrapes and bumps. Care of a team of wagon horses is a lot of work.

Most wagon outfits travel with 12 to 17 thoroughbreds in the stable. These high-spirited racing machines require high octane food – oats, hay, vitamins, and other tasty things a couple times a day. A team of first-string wagon horses can eat their way through a lot of mighty expensive oats on their summer racing diet.

In spite of the years that go into training wagon racing thoroughbreds, not everything always goes exactly according to plan. The horses may be brilliant, but they're not robots. Occasionally, they will stray out of a racing lane. Alas, that's a five-second penalty a virtual guarantee that the team will lose the race.

**Glen Ridsdale (in black) and Bert Croteau (in red) strain to keep control of their horses as Jim Nevada's stray out of their lane. Calgary Stampede, July 8, 2000. (PAUL EASTON PHOTO)**

Human sports stars hit the goal post, strike out, slice, and crash. So why can't a wagon horse make an occasional wrong turn?

**John Lumsden's horses turn too soon. Trout Springs, June 20, 1993.** (PAUL EASTON PHOTO)

Slips and spills are inevitable. By the time the reins are untangled, the drivers, outriders, and horses are all wearing a lot of dirt.

Yes, there is some risk for the horses of wagon racing. The SPCA watches over them, the animal rights activists want to "save" them. There are a few horse injuries, which happens if you live to run. But statistically, more horses are injured in the off-season while they're running free in the fields than during the races. Gopher holes on the range are more perilous than a groomed wagon track.

Many wagon racing thoroughbreds are refugees from other horse racing events. Here they are given new life as wagon stars, where they can run as long as they're able, some as long as 15 years. If only horses could talk. . . .

**A wagon comes to an abrupt stop, and driver Phil Pollack swings wide to avoid contact. The mishap only looks bad. One lead horse lost his footing, his teammates fell down with him, and the wagon came to a very abrupt halt. No serious injuries. Trout Springs, June 19, 1993. (PAUL EASTON PHOTO)**

For some equestrian champions, fitted, monogrammed horse blankets and 747 transport are *de rigueur*. Not here. But what these horses lives may lack in unnecessary grandeur is more than made up by the love and caring they receive from their owners.

Seeing them in their corral outside the wagon trailer village, it's hard to believe that many of these beauties were throwaways from regular horse racing. Warm twilight in the foothills isn't any kind of glue factory.

**After the race. Strathmore, August 3, 1997. (CAROL EASTON PHOTO)**

As the chuckwagons move on to races in another city, camp is broken and set up again. Each time, after the horses are offloaded, portable barns are set up, and all the remaining space is divided into a patchwork of impromptu corrals for all those horses – a mobile ranch.

**The Glass family's wagon outfit barns. These painted racing wagons are traditional round-up wagons that adhere precisely to racing specifications. The box is wood with square corners, 11 feet 4 inches longs, 58 inches wide, and 24 inches deep. Bashaw, June 1996. (PAUL EASTON PHOTO)**

Repairing a wheel, a mundane but important task. Wagon wheels have been known to fall off during the race. Ponoka Stampede, June 29, 1996.
(PAUL EASTON PHOTO)

A crew member finds another use for a saddle pad. Midafternoon is down-time for horses and crew. Maintenance is finished, and it's not time yet to think about the race this evening. Ponoka Stampede, June 27, 1997.
(PAUL EASTON PHOTO)

Then there are the chuckwagons. A contemporary racing chuckwagon is a speed-optimized descendant of the original "chuck" wagon, a mobile pantry and kitchen created in the 1860s to feed cowboys on the range. According to cowboy folklore, after a roundup, chuckwagons from neighboring ranches would race to the nearest saloon, where the loser would buy the first round.

In 1923, Guy Weadick used wagon racing as the centerpiece of a Wild West celebration that lives on in the world-famous Rangeland Derby of the Calgary Stampede and in countless other rodeos and wagon races across the West. Of course, now that chuckwagons are driven by accredited professionals, a winning wagon driver gets more than a free drink!

Push! Loading Buddy Bensmiller's wagon. High River, June 1992. (PAUL EASTON PHOTO)

Buddy Bensmiller carries his hook-up harnesses. In the world of chuckwagon racing, the barn crew isn't expected to do everything. Even champion chuckwagon drivers carry their own gear and help hook the team to the wagon. Lethbridge, June 1999. (PAUL EASTON PHOTO)

Modern chuckwagon racing is a rite of summer throughout western Canada and the northwestern United States. Each week, the racers move to a new location on the circuit. The wagons, personnel, equipment, horses, and supplies are continually in transit. Custom-built semitrailers with canvas sidewalls fold out into portable barns.

The wagons are racing machines. Safe race-day performance demands the same obsessive maintenance that goes into auto racing . But these cowboys don't change spark plugs and tune engines. After they finish greasing the axle for this wagon wheel, they'll need to feed the horses – again.

The barn crew works hard. The wagon must be cleaned, the tack must be polished, and horse washing and brushing never seems to end. It's exhausting.

An old cowboy adage (taken from Texas Bix Bender's *Don't Squat with Yer Spurs On!*) applies to modern wagon racing: "If you expect to follow the trail, you must do your sleepin' in the winter." Or try to catch some catnaps whenever you can!

When the day is done, everything must be packed and loaded for the trip to the next race on the circuit. Removal of the driver, tarp, and stove doesn't shed much weight when preparing a chuckwagon for transit. Fully loaded the wagon is 1325 pounds. Empty and ready for transit it's about 1000 pounds. This is serious luggage.

When the last day of racing is done, everyone breaks camp immedi- ately. It's a tradition to move on and set up at the next city, even when that requires traveling through the night.

Family and accommodation moves out. The barn crew, the horses, and their gear travel in an 18-wheeler, which has served as a portable barn. Together the wagon teams form a caravan en route to the next race.

**The Willard racing team hits the road. The wagon is in the back, home is trailing along behind. High River, June 1992. (CAROL EASTON PHOTO)**

## CHAPTER SIX

# THE FAMILIES & FANS
## Steadfast, Devoted & Exuberant

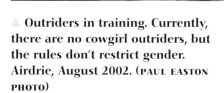

*T*OURISTS VIEWING THEIR FIRST WAGON RACE SEE ONLY THE SPECTACLE OF the race and a few drivers. But real fans know that chuckwagon racing is a people sport. The driver has likely been coached by his father or uncle, his son is often outriding, and everybody in his extended family helps out before and after the race. This family may include a few adoptees, such as long-time outriders, or maybe even some city folk who only intended to sponsor a wagon for a couple of races but got hooked on the lifestyle.

The families of chuckwagon racing need to be tightly knit. During racing season, they come together from distant locales to pursue a common passion. They travel together for months at a time and live in close quarters. The children grow up understanding this itinerant life, and may marry their childhood playmates. In times of injury and tragedy, which are part of the sport, the families are there for one another. And when it's time to celebrate, there's plenty of company.

The fans in the grandstand are as likely to be local ranch hands as big-city oil company executives. But when the race is over and the tourists leave, the real devotees head for the barns. After each race, the season-long tailgate party continues. The tack is hanging on the canvas barn, the horses mill about in the background. Pull up a hay bale and have a refreshment.

Often the fans support chuckwagon racing with more than just loud cheers. They put their money where their mouths are. Wagon tarps are emblazoned with the international trademarks of manufacturers of everything from cars to jeans to snuff to motorhomes. These "city folk" make it all possible. Millionaire weekend cowboys can be seen hangin' out in the barns. "Them's pretty fancy boots – careful where y'all step."

▲ Outriders in training. Currently, there are no cowgirl outriders, but the rules don't restrict gender. Airdrie, August 2002. (PAUL EASTON PHOTO)

◀ The reins for the family wagon are frequently passed from father to son. Their fathers (left to right) Ward Willard, Herman Flad, Reg Johnstone, and Tom Glass. Together they have amassed 108 years of experience racing chuckwagons. Their sons (left to right) Troy Flad, Jason Glass, Jason Johnstone, and Jess Willard. Strathmore, August 1997. (CAROL EASTON PHOTO)

It's not just the driver and his horses that are excited at the home-stretch. Each season, the employees of corporate sponsors band together to support their chuckwagon. Naturally, effective support requires attendance at races with friends and family, judicious partying, and rousing cheers as your wagon streaks for the finish line.

**Driver Norm Cuthbertson kisses his new wife, Judy. This chuckwagon smooch offers a glimpse into the life of the wagon community – you can see how wedded they are to their sport! Before promotion to Mrs., this lovely bride was the groom's barn manager. A wedding in the barn seems only proper. Calgary Stampede, July 1996. (PAUL EASTON PHOTO)**

Guarding the water. This young cowboy has on his fancy duds for a little fun after the races. But first he has to make sure his family's wagon horses don't drink too much water too quickly. He already understands the old cowboy adage, "Nothin's better than a cool drink of water — but too much can give you a bellyache." High River, 1993. (PAUL EASTON PHOTO)

An avid chuckwagon fan behind the infield fence. This devotee, racing sheet in hand, has poached a photographer's perch. Odds are the remainder of this race will be photographed without the use of the stool. Strathmore, August 5, 2000. (CAROL EASTON PHOTO)

When an entire corporation identifies with a wagon racing team, a rodeo and wagon race on a summer weekend is a dandy place for a picnic with clowns and hot dogs for the kids. In some cities, including Calgary, the chuckwagon races are the highlight of the summer rodeo and stampede. Everybody gets in on the act.

**TransAlta fans cheer at the finish line. Calgary Stampede, July 11, 1995. (PAUL EASTON PHOTO)**

A very young fan learns all about the family tradition of chuckwagon racing. Calgary Stampede, July 4, 1992. (PAUL EASTON PHOTO)

These "Chicks" are prominent professional women who use their chuckwagon (well, actually, their chickwagon) as the focus of their charitable and community service. Seen here in finely tailored attire, they are rooting for their wagon, which tonight is up against the entry from Hooters. Calgary Stampede, July 8, 2000. (CAROL EASTON PHOTO)

Employees of Stampeder Exploration cheer at the company bleacher alongside the annual Calgary Stampede parade. These folks are working – a nice job if you can get it. Calgary Stampede, July 4, 1997. (PAUL EASTON PHOTO)

Fans on horseback. High River, August 25, 2001. (CAROL EASTON PHOTO)

To the uninitiated visitor, it's Cowboy Mardi Gras. Hotels are full, volunteers in Stetsons greet visitors at the airport, storefronts are decorated, employees wear cowboy duds, department stores and politicians host pancake breakfasts. And not a lot of work gets done as the whole town turns out to celebrate western heritage.

Long-time sponsors are adopted into the sport. Many return to sponsor the same wagon outfit year after year, bidding at auction for the right to sponsor a "tarp." Some sponsors become much more than financial benefactors and develop a deep emotional attachment to the families, their horses and the sport.

**Here, the cowboy, Troy Dorchester, with his hands folded is the driver. The dude on the left, Bill Singh, driving the wagon after the race, has a much different job description: he usually runs the sponsoring company. Ponoka Stampede, July 1997. (PAUL EASTON PHOTO)**

# CHAPTER SEVEN

# THE RACE
## *Setting Up for the Stretch Drive*

**C**OMING AROUND THE THIRD CORNER, DRIVERS PREPARE FOR THE SPRINT to the finish. Each driver must now consider his position on the track because after the fourth corner he must commit to a lane for the home-stretch. If there is anything in reserve, now is the time to open up. If there is an opening, watch for a veteran driver to sneak through and find an open line to the finish. About 60 seconds have elapsed. In another 20 seconds or so, the race will be over.

At the same time, the driver must be aware of the position of his out-riders on the track. If they are close by, he can proceed full throttle. But if his outriders haven't been able to catch up, he must pull back on the reins and slow down a bit because if the outriders are more than 150 feet behind the wagon when it crosses the finish line, the team will incur steep time penalties and an almost certain loss.

All the while, the grandstand is getting closer, and it's hard to hear anything above the roar of the crowd. Spectators, sponsors, and families scream last minute exhortations.

The most extreme emotions in the race seem to be expressed about now. The finish line is almost is coming in sight. The finish line camera and judges await. Like so many other races, after five-eights of a mile, this race may be won by a horse's nose.

**Jess Williard turns for home.
Ponoka Stampede, August 2, 1998.**
(CAROL EASTON PHOTO)

**Jerry Bremner lets out a yell as he navigates the third corner.
Calgary Stampede, July 16, 2000.**
(PAUL EASTON PHOTO)

In these last few extreme seconds, with victory hanging in the balance, the differing signature styles of the drivers are obvious. Some drivers yell, others whistle, a few toss the reins. Actually, it probably doesn't matter. The horses already know to give it their all.

**Reg Johnstone (in black), Leo Tournier (in white), and Doug Irvine (in yellow). Calgary Stampede, July 7, 2000.** (CAROL EASTON PHOTO)

Last minute encouragement. Jess Willard (in red), Doug Irvine (in black), and Ross Knight (in yellow). Calgary Stampede, July 16, 2000. (CAROL EASTON PHOTO)

This veteran cowboy has found a beautiful line through the corner, going wide, then cutting back into the rail. In another few seconds, he'll be on the fourth corner, where he can choose the rail lane and stay there to the finish line. Herman Flad. Lethbridge, June 18, 1999. (PAUL EASTON PHOTO)

After three quarters of the race, two wagons are in a dead heat. The track is heavy, and apparently rail position didn't matter. They are setting up for a drag race to the finish line. But there are only two red shirted and white shirted outriders in sight. Dennis MacGillvary (in red) and Edgar Baptiste (in white) run neck-and-neck. Calgary Stampede, July 6, 1998. (PAUL EASTON PHOTO)

Coming down the home stretch, the race is into the last 10 seconds. No more time for strategy now. It's pull out and pass or settle for second place – and no driver ever likes to settle for second.

Now that they've rounded the fourth corner and set up for the stretch drive, the finish line and the screaming crowd in the grandstand are in sight. The sound is deafening. These are veteran professional drivers, and this is supposed to be just another race. But just look at the emotion they express. Jason Glass (in black) and Mike Vigen (in white). Strathmore, August 5, 1995. (PAUL EASTON PHOTO)

Of course, you don't have to yell to convey emotion, Jake Friesen (in black) and Leonard DeLaronde (in white) leave Don Chapin (in yellow) and Troy Flad (in red) in the dust. Strathmore, August 2, 1998. (CAROL EASTON PHOTO)

It's now past the time to worry about the outriders. They'll just have to get to the finish on time. And the speed of the other wagons doesn't matter either. What matters is just this wagon and this team. Light the afterburners. Can't we go just a little bit faster, PLEASE?

Kelly Sutherland heads for home. Kelly's not hiding his face. He's not shy. This is the signature manoeuvre of a champion driver a few feet from the finish line. Trout Springs, June 1993. (CAROL EASTON PHOTO)

It's a pity horses can't talk. After years of wagon racing experience, their commentary would be terrific. Something like "Relax, boss. Enjoy the ride. Wave at the crowd in the grandstand. We'll take it home from here. We're headed for another perfect finish."

**Another style for the same effect. Every driver has his own way of encouraging his steeds with the finish line is in sight. This is a fourth generation Wagon racer, with a family legacy of chuckwagon knowledge to refine his technique. But these horses already know what to do. They've got it "wide open." Colt Cosgrave's wheels are on fire as he outraces Jess Willard. Medicine Hat, June 12, 1999. (CAROL EASTON PHOTO)**

With the outriders close by, this race is won. Jerry Bremner just over the finish line. Calgary Stampede, July 1992. (PAUL EASTON PHOTO)

Jim Nevada (in white) takes it standing up over Jerry Bremner (in red) and Luke Tournier (in black). Calgary Stampede, July 13, 2000. (CAROL EASTON PHOTO)

And, after about 80 seconds, the finish line is crossed. Another race is over.

**Wayne Knight flies past the flag. Calgary Stampede, July 11, 2000.**
(PAUL EASTON PHOTO)

*Paul & Carol Easton*

Drag racers have parachutes to slow them down. In wagon racing, the horses may continue halfway around the track before the adrenaline rushing through their veins abates enough for them to stop.

**Slowing down after the finish line. Cam Shaurette (in white) and Floyd Bradshaw (in red) are almost obscured by all the mud they've kicked up. Ponoka Stampede, June 28, 1998. (CAROL EASTON PHOTO)**

That's the end of the wagon race as seen through the camera lens. Hope you enjoyed the ride!

Of course, if you really want to see these horses, meet the cowboys and their families, and feel the thunder, you'll need to be here in person. So, y'all come down to the wagon races, hear? But before you jump into your pickup, check the web sites at www.wpca.com and www.cpcaracing.com for the racing schedules of the World Professional Chuckwagon Association and Canadian Professional Chuckwagon Association. And when you get there, expect to meet wagon fans from across the country and around the world.

See you at the races!

**This shot at sunset evokes a line from Ian Tyson's "Half a Mile of Hell," which is usually played for the grandstand each evening. Norm Cuthbertson salutes the crowd. Calgary Stampede, July 11, 1995. (CAROL EASTON PHOTO)**